D0293854

Draft

TREATY
ESTABLISHING A

CONSTITUTION FOR EUROPE

SUBMITTED TO THE
EUROPEAN COUNCIL MEETING IN
THESSALONIKI

—— *20 June 2003* ——

the european convention

**Europe Direct is a service to help you find answers
to your questions about the European Union**

**New freephone number:
00 800 6 7 8 9 10 11**

A great deal of additional information on the European Union
is available on the Internet. It can be accessed through the Europa server
(http://europa.eu.int).

Cataloguing data can be found at the end of this publication.

Luxembourg: Office for Official Publications of the European Communities, 2003

ISBN 92-78-40171-4

PREFACE

Noting that the European Union was coming to a turning point in its existence, the European Council which met in Laeken, Belgium, on 14 and 15 December 2001 convened the European Convention on the future of Europe.

The Convention was asked to draw up proposals on three subjects: how to bring citizens closer to the European design and European Institutions; how to organise politics and the European political area in an enlarged Union; and how to develop the Union into a stabilising factor and a model in the new world order.

The Convention has identified responses to the questions put in the Laeken declaration:

- it proposes a better division of Union and Member State competences;
- it recommends a merger of the Treaties and the attribution of legal personality to the Union;
- it establishes a simplification of the Union's instruments of action;
- it proposes measures to increase the democracy, transparency and efficiency of the European Union, by developing the contribution of national Parliaments to the legitimacy of the European design, by simplifying the decision-making processes, and by making the functioning of the European Institutions more transparent and comprehensible;
- it establishes the necessary measures to improve the structure and enhance the role of each of the Union's three ins-

titutions, taking account, in particular, of the consequences of enlargement.

The Laeken declaration also asked whether the simplification and reorganisation of the Treaties should not pave the way for the adoption of a constitutional text. The Convention's proceedings ultimately led to the drawing up of a draft Constitution for Europe, which achieved a broad consensus at the plenary session on 13 June 2003.

That is the text which it is our privilege to present today, 20 June 2003, to the European Council meeting in Thessaloniki, on behalf of the European Convention, in the hope that it will constitute the foundation of a future Treaty establishing the European Constitution.

Valéry Giscard d'Estaing
President of the Convention

Giuliano Amato
Vice-President

Jean-Luc Dehaene
Vice-President

DRAFT

TREATY ESTABLISHING A CONSTITUTION FOR EUROPE

PREAMBLE

DRAFT TREATY

Χρώμεθα γὰρ πολιτείᾳ... καὶ ὄνομα μὲν διὰ τὸ μὴ ἐς ὀλίγους ἀλλ᾽ ἐς πλείονας οἰκεῖν δημοκρατία κέκληται.

Our Constitution ... is called a democracy because power is in the hands not of a minority but of the greatest number.

Thucydides II, 37

Conscious that Europe is a continent that has brought forth civilisation; that its inhabitants, arriving in successive waves since the first ages of mankind, have gradually developed the values underlying humanism: equality of persons, freedom, respect for reason,

Drawing inspiration from the cultural, religious and humanist inheritance of Europe, the values of which, still present in its heritage, have embedded within the life of society its perception of the central role of the human person and his or her inviolable and inalienable rights, and of respect for law,

Believing that reunited Europe intends to continue along this path of civilisation, progress and prosperity, for the good of all its inhabitants, including the weakest and most deprived; that it wishes to remain a continent open to culture, learning and social progress; and that it wishes to deepen the democratic and transparent nature of its public life, and to strive for peace, justice and solidarity throughout the world,

Convinced that, while remaining proud of their own national identities and history, the peoples of Europe are determined to transcend their ancient divisions and, united ever more closely, to forge a common destiny,

Convinced that, thus 'united in its diversity', Europe offers them the best chance of pursuing, with due regard for the rights of each individual and in awareness of their responsibilities towards future generations and the Earth, the great venture which makes of it a special area of human hope,

Grateful to the members of the European Convention for having prepared this Constitution on behalf of the citizens and States of Europe,

[Who, having exchanged their full powers, found in good and due form, have agreed as follows:]

PART I

Title I	DEFINITION AND OBJECTIVES OF THE UNION

Article 1   ESTABLISHMENT OF THE UNION

1.   Reflecting the will of the citizens and States of Europe to build a common future, this Constitution establishes the European Union, on which the Member States confer competences to attain objectives they have in common. The Union shall coordinate the policies by which the Member States aim to achieve these objectives, and shall exercise in the Community way the competences they confer on it.

2.   The Union shall be open to all European States which respect its values and are committed to promoting them together.

Article 2   THE UNION'S VALUES

The Union is founded on the values of respect for human dignity, liberty, democracy, equality, the rule of law and respect for human rights. These values are common to the Member States in a society of pluralism, tolerance, justice, solidarity and non-discrimination.

Article 3   THE UNION'S OBJECTIVES

1.   The Union's aim is to promote peace, its values and the well-being of its peoples.

2.   The Union shall offer its citizens an area of freedom, security and justice without internal frontiers, and a single market where competition is free and undistorted.

3.   The Union shall work for a Europe of sustainable development based on balanced economic growth, a social market economy, highly competitive and aiming at full employment and social progress, and with a high level of protection and improvement of the quality of the environment. It shall promote scientific and technological advance.

It shall combat social exclusion and discrimination, and shall promote social justice and protection, equality between women and men, solidarity between generations and protection of children's rights.

It shall promote economic, social and territorial cohesion, and solidarity among Member States.

The Union shall respect its rich cultural and linguistic diversity, and shall ensure that Europe's cultural heritage is safeguarded and enhanced.

4.   In its relations with the wider world, the Union shall uphold and promote its values and interests. It shall contribute to peace, security, the sustainable development of the earth, solidarity and mutual respect among peoples, free and fair trade, eradication of poverty and protection of human rights and in particular children's rights, as well as to strict observance and development of international law, including respect for the principles of the United Nations Charter.

5.   These objectives shall be pursued by appropriate means, depending on the extent to which the relevant competences are attributed to the Union in this Constitution.

Article 4   FUNDAMENTAL FREEDOMS AND NON-DISCRIMINATION

1.   Free movement of persons, goods, services and capital, and freedom of establishment shall be guaranteed within and by the Union, in accordance with the provisions of this Constitution.

2.   In the field of application of this Constitution, and without prejudice to any of its specific provisions, any discrimination on grounds of nationality shall be prohibited.

Article 5   RELATIONS BETWEEN THE UNION AND THE MEMBER STATES

1.   The Union shall respect the national identities of its Member States, inherent in their fundamental structures, political and constitutional, inclusive of regional and local self-government. It shall respect their essential State functions, including those for ensuring the territorial integrity of the State, and for maintaining law and order and safeguarding internal security.

2.   Following the principle of loyal cooperation, the Union and the Member States shall, in full mutual respect, assist each other in carrying out tasks which flow from the Constitution.

The Member States shall facilitate the achievement of the Union's tasks and refrain from any measure which could jeopardise the attainment of the objectives set out in the Constitution.

Article 6   LEGAL PERSONALITY

The Union shall have legal personality.

| Title II | FUNDAMENTAL RIGHTS AND CITIZENSHIP OF THE UNION |

Title II   # FUNDAMENTAL RIGHTS AND CITIZENSHIP OF THE UNION

Article 7   ## FUNDAMENTAL RIGHTS

1.   The Union shall recognise the rights, freedoms and principles set out in the Charter of Fundamental Rights which constitutes Part II of this Constitution.

2.   The Union shall seek accession to the European Convention for the Protection of Human Rights and Fundamental Freedoms. Accession to that Convention shall not affect the Union's competences as defined in this Constitution.

3.   Fundamental rights, as guaranteed by the European Convention for the Protection of Human Rights and Fundamental Freedoms, and as they result from the constitutional traditions common to the Member States, shall constitute general principles of the Union's law.

Article 8   ## CITIZENSHIP OF THE UNION

1.   Every national of a Member State shall be a citizen of the Union. Citizenship of the Union shall be additional to national citizenship; it shall not replace it.

2.　　　　　　　Citizens of the Union shall enjoy the rights and be subject to the duties provided for in this Constitution. They shall have:

- the right to move and reside freely within the territory of the Member States;
- the right to vote and to stand as candidates in elections to the European Parliament and in municipal elections in their Member State of residence, under the same conditions as nationals of that State;
- the right to enjoy, in the territory of a third country in which the Member State of which they are nationals is not represented, the protection of the diplomatic and consular authorities of any Member State on the same conditions as the nationals of that State;
- the right to petition the European Parliament, to apply to the European Ombudsman, and to write to the Institutions and advisory bodies of the Union in any of the Constitution's languages and to obtain a reply in the same language.

3.　　　　　　　These rights shall be exercised in accordance with the conditions and limits defined by this Constitution and by the measures adopted to give it effect.

Title III   UNION COMPETENCES

Article 9   FUNDAMENTAL PRINCIPLES

1.   The limits of Union competences are governed by the principle of conferral. The use of Union competences is governed by the principles of subsidiarity and proportionality.

2.   Under the principle of conferral, the Union shall act within the limits of the competences conferred upon it by the Member States in the Constitution to attain the objectives set out in the Constitution. Competences not conferred upon the Union in the Constitution remain with the Member States.

3.   Under the principle of subsidiarity, in areas which do not fall within its exclusive competence the Union shall act only if and insofar as the objectives of the intended action cannot be sufficiently achieved by the Member States, either at central level or at regional and local level, but can rather, by reason of the scale or effects of the proposed action, be better achieved at Union level.

The Union Institutions shall apply the principle of subsidiarity as laid down in the Protocol on the application of the principles of subsidiarity and proportionality, annexed to the Constitution. National Parliaments shall ensure compliance with that principle in accordance with the procedure set out in the Protocol.

4.   Under the principle of proportionality, the content and form of Union action shall not exceed what is necessary to achieve the objectives of the Constitution.

The Institutions shall apply the principle of proportionality as laid down in the Protocol referred to in paragraph 3.

Article 10   UNION LAW

1.   The Constitution, and law adopted by the Union's Institutions in exercising competences conferred on it, shall have primacy over the law of the Member States.

2.   Member States shall take all appropriate measures, general or particular, to ensure fulfilment of the obligations flowing from the Constitution or resulting from the Union Institutions' acts.

Article 11   CATEGORIES OF COMPETENCE

1.   When the Constitution confers on the Union exclusive competence in a specific area, only the Union may legislate and adopt legally binding acts, the Member States being able to do so themselves only if so empowered by the Union or for the implementation of acts adopted by the Union.

2. When the Constitution confers on the Union a competence shared with the Member States in a specific area, the Union and the Member States shall have the power to legislate and adopt legally binding acts in that area. The Member States shall exercise their competence to the extent that the Union has not exercised, or has decided to cease exercising, its competence.

3. The Union shall have competence to promote and coordinate the economic and employment policies of the Member States.

4. The Union shall have competence to define and implement a common foreign and security policy, including the progressive framing of a common defence policy.

5. In certain areas and in the conditions laid down in the Constitution, the Union shall have competence to carry out actions to support, coordinate or supplement the actions of the Member States, without thereby superseding their competence in these areas.

6. The scope of and arrangements for exercising the Union's competences shall be determined by the provisions specific to each area in Part III.

Article 12   EXCLUSIVE COMPETENCE

1.   The Union shall have exclusive competence to establish the competition rules necessary for the functioning of the internal market, and in the following areas:

- monetary policy, for the Member States which have adopted the euro,
- common commercial policy,
- customs union,
- the conservation of marine biological resources under the common fisheries policy.

2.   The Union shall have exclusive competence for the conclusion of an international agreement when its conclusion is provided for in a legislative act of the Union, is necessary to enable the Union to exercise its competence internally, or affects an internal Union act.

Article 13   AREAS OF SHARED COMPETENCE

1.   The Union shall share competence with the Member States where the Constitution confers on it a competence which does not relate to the areas referred to in Articles 12 and 16.

2. Shared competence applies in the following principal areas:

- internal market,
- area of freedom, security and justice,
- agriculture and fisheries, excluding the conservation of marine biological resources,
- transport and trans-European networks,
- energy,
- social policy, for aspects defined in Part III,
- economic, social and territorial cohesion,
- environment,
- consumer protection,
- common safety concerns in public health matters.

3. In the areas of research, technological development and space, the Union shall have competence to carry out actions, in particular to define and implement programmes; however, the exercise of that competence may not result in Member States being prevented from exercising theirs.

4. In the areas of development cooperation and humanitarian aid, the Union shall have competence to take action and conduct a common policy; however, the exercise of that competence may not result in Member States being prevented from exercising theirs.

Article 14   THE COORDINATION OF ECONOMIC
AND EMPLOYMENT POLICIES

1.   The Union shall adopt measures to ensure coordination of the economic policies of the Member States, in particular by adopting broad guidelines for these policies. The Member States shall coordinate their economic policies within the Union.

2.   Specific provisions shall apply to those Member States which have adopted the euro.

3.   The Union shall adopt measures to ensure coordination of the employment policies of the Member States, in particular by adopting guidelines for these policies.

4.   The Union may adopt initiatives to ensure coordination of Member States' social policies.

Article 15   THE COMMON FOREIGN AND
SECURITY POLICY

1.   The Union's competence in matters of common foreign and security policy shall cover all areas of foreign policy and all questions relating to the Union's security, including the progressive framing of a common defence policy, which might lead to a common defence.

2.   Member States shall actively and unreservedly support the Union's common foreign and security policy in a spirit of loyalty and mutual solidarity and shall comply with the acts adopted by the Union in this area. They shall refrain from action contrary to the Union's interests or likely to impair its effectiveness.

Article 16   AREAS OF SUPPORTING,
                COORDINATING OR COMPLEMENTARY
                ACTION

1.   The Union may take supporting, coordinating or complementary action.

2.   The areas for supporting, coordinating or complementary action shall be, at European level:

- industry
- protection and improvement of human health
- education, vocational training, youth and sport
- culture
- civil protection.

3.   Legally binding acts adopted by the Union on the basis of the provisions specific to these areas in Part III may not entail harmonisation of Member States' laws or regulations.

Article 17   FLEXIBILITY CLAUSE

1.   If action by the Union should prove necessary within the framework of the policies defined in Part III to attain one of the objectives set by the Constitution, and the Constitution has not provided the necessary powers, the Council of Ministers, acting unanimously on a proposal from the Commission and after obtaining the consent of the European Parliament, shall take the appropriate measures.

2.   Using the procedure for monitoring the subsidiarity principle referred to in Article 9(3), the Commission shall draw Member States' national Parliaments' attention to proposals based on this Article.

3.   Provisions adopted on the basis of this Article may not entail harmonisation of Member States' laws or regulations in cases where the Constitution excludes such harmonisation.

| *Title IV* | # THE UNION'S INSTITUTIONS |

| *Chapter I* | ## INSTITUTIONAL FRAMEWORK |

| *Article 18* | ### THE UNION'S INSTITUTIONS |

1. The Union shall be served by a single institutional framework which shall aim to:

- advance the objectives of the Union,
- promote the values of the Union,
- serve the interests of the Union, its citizens and its Member States,

and ensure the consistency, effectiveness and continuity of the policies and actions which it undertakes in pursuit of its objectives.

2. This institutional framework comprises:

The European Parliament,
The European Council,
The Council of Ministers,
The European Commission,
The Court of Justice.

3. Each Institution shall act within the limits of the powers conferred on it in the Constitution, and in conformity with the procedures and conditions set out in it. The Institutions shall practice full mutual cooperation.

Article 19   THE EUROPEAN PARLIAMENT

1. The European Parliament shall, jointly with the Council of Ministers, enact legislation, and exercise the budgetary function, as well as functions of political control and consultation as laid down in the Constitution. It shall elect the President of the European Commission.

2. The European Parliament shall be elected by direct universal suffrage of European citizens in free and secret ballot for a term of five years. Its members shall not exceed seven hundred and thirty-six in number. Representation of European citizens shall be degressively proportional, with a minimum threshold of four members per Member State.

Sufficiently in advance of the European Parliamentary elections in 2009, and, as necessary thereafter for further elections, the European Council shall adopt by unanimity, on the basis of a proposal from the European Parliament and with its consent, a decision establishing the composition of the European Parliament, respecting the principles set out above.

3.   The European Parliament shall elect its President and its officers from among its members.

Article 20   THE EUROPEAN COUNCIL

1.   The European Council shall provide the Union with the necessary impetus for its development, and shall define its general political directions and priorities. It does not exercise legislative functions.

2.   The European Council shall consist of the Heads of State or Government of the Member States, together with its President and the President of the Commission. The Union Minister for Foreign Affairs shall take part in its work.

3.   The European Council shall meet quarterly, convened by its President. When the agenda so requires, its members may decide to be assisted by a minister and, in the case of the President of the Commission, a European Commissioner. When the situation so requires, the President shall convene a special meeting of the European Council.

4.   Except where the Constitution provides otherwise, decisions of the European Council shall be taken by consensus.

Article 21　　THE EUROPEAN COUNCIL CHAIR

1.　　　　The European Council shall elect its President, by qualified majority, for a term of two and a half years, renewable once. In the event of an impediment or serious misconduct, the European Council can end his or her mandate according to the same procedure.

2.　　　　The President of the European Council:

- shall chair it and drive forward its work,
- shall ensure its proper preparation and continuity in cooperation with the President of the Commission, and on the basis of the work of the General Affairs Council,
- shall endeavour to facilitate cohesion and consensus within the European Council,
- shall present a report to the European Parliament after each of its meetings.

The President of the European Council shall at his or her level and in that capacity ensure the external representation of the Union on issues concerning its common foreign and security policy, without prejudice to the responsibilities of the Union Minister for Foreign Affairs.

3.　　　　The President of the European Council may not hold a national mandate.

Article 22   THE COUNCIL OF MINISTERS

1.   The Council of Ministers shall, jointly with the European Parliament, enact legislation, exercise the budgetary function and carry out policy-making and coordinating functions, as laid down in the Constitution.

2.   The Council of Ministers shall consist of a representative of each Member State at ministerial level for each of its formations. Only this representative may commit the Member State in question and cast its vote.

3.   Except where the Constitution provides otherwise, decisions of the Council of Ministers shall be taken by qualified majority.

Article 23   FORMATIONS OF THE
               COUNCIL OF MINISTERS

1.   The Legislative and General Affairs Council shall ensure consistency in the work of the Council of Ministers.

When it acts in its General Affairs function, it shall, in liaison with the Commission, prepare, and ensure follow-up to, meetings of the European Council.

When it acts in its legislative function, the Council of Ministers shall consider and, jointly with the European Parliament, enact

European laws and European framework laws, in accordance with the provisions of the Constitution. In this function, each Member State's representation shall include one or two representatives at ministerial level with relevant expertise, reflecting the business on the agenda of the Council of Ministers.

2. The Foreign Affairs Council shall, on the basis of strategic guidelines laid down by the European Council, flesh out the Union's external policies, and ensure that its actions are consistent. It shall be chaired by the Union Minister for Foreign Affairs.

3. The European Council shall adopt a European decision establishing further formations in which the Council of Ministers may meet.

4. The Presidency of Council of Ministers formations, other than that of Foreign Affairs, shall be held by Member State representatives within the Council of Ministers on the basis of equal rotation for periods of at least a year. The European Council shall adopt a European decision establishing the rules of such rotation, taking into account European political and geographical balance and the diversity of Member States.

Article 24   QUALIFIED MAJORITY

1. When the European Council or the Council of Ministers takes decisions by qualified majority, such a major-

ity shall consist of the majority of Member States, representing at least three fifths of the population of the Union.

2.   When the Constitution does not require the European Council or the Council of Ministers to act on the basis of a proposal of the Commission, or when the European Council or the Council of Ministers is not acting on the initiative of the Union Minister for Foreign Affairs, the required qualified majority shall consist of two thirds of the Member States, representing at least three fifths of the population of the Union.

3.   The provisions of paragraphs 1 and 2 shall take effect on 1 November 2009, after the European Parliament elections have taken place, according to the provisions of Article 19.

4.   Where the Constitution provides in Part III for European laws and framework laws to be adopted by the Council of Ministers according to a special legislative procedure, the European Council can adopt, on its own initiative and by unanimity, after a period of consideration of at least six months, a decision allowing for the adoption of such European laws or framework laws according to the ordinary legislative procedure. The European Council shall act after consulting the European Parliament and informing the national Parliaments.

Where the Constitution provides in Part III for the Council of Ministers to act unanimously in a given area, the European

Council can adopt, on its own initiative and by unanimity, a European decision allowing the Council of Ministers to act by qualified majority in that area. Any initiative taken by the European Council under this subparagraph shall be sent to national Parliaments no less than four months before any decision is taken on it.

5.   Within the European Council, its President and the President of the Commission do not vote.

Article 25   THE EUROPEAN COMMISSION

1.   The European Commission shall promote the general European interest and take appropriate initiatives to that end. It shall ensure the application of the Constitution, and steps taken by the Institutions under the Constitution. It shall oversee the application of Union law under the control of the Court of Justice. It shall execute the budget and manage programmes. It shall exercise coordinating, executive and management functions, as laid down in the Constitution. With the exception of the common foreign and security policy, and other cases provided for in the Constitution, it shall ensure the Union's external representation. It shall initiate the Union's annual and multiannual programming with a view to achieving interinstitutional agreements.

2.   Except where the Constitution provides otherwise, Union legislative acts can be adopted only on the basis of

a Commission proposal. Other acts are adopted on the basis of a Commission proposal where the Constitution so provides.

3.   The Commission shall consist of a College comprising its President, the Union Minister of Foreign Affairs/Vice-President, and thirteen European Commissioners selected on the basis of a system of equal rotation between the Member States. This system shall be established by a European decision adopted by the European Council on the basis of the following principles:

> *(a)* Member States shall be treated on a strictly equal footing as regard determination of the sequence of, and the time spent by, their nationals as Members of the College; consequently, the difference between the total number of terms of office held by nationals of any given pair of Member States may never be more than one;
>
> *(b)* subject to point (a), each successive College shall be so composed as to reflect satisfactorily the demographic and geographical range of all the Member States of the Union.

The Commission President shall appoint non-voting Commissioners, chosen according to the same criteria as apply for Members of the College and coming from all other Member States.

These arrangements shall take effect on 1 November 2009.

4. In carrying out its responsibilities, the Commission shall be completely independent. In the discharge of their duties, the European Commissioners and Commissioners shall neither seek nor take instructions from any government or other body.

5. The Commission, as a College, shall be responsible to the European Parliament. The Commission President shall be responsible to the European Parliament for the activities of the Commissioners. Under the procedures set out in Article III-243, the European Parliament may pass a censure motion on the Commission. If such a motion is passed, the European Commissioners and Commissioners must all resign. The Commission shall continue to handle everyday business until a new College is nominated.

Article 26 THE PRESIDENT OF THE
EUROPEAN COMMISSION

1. Taking into account the elections to the European Parliament and after appropriate consultations, the European Council, deciding by qualified majority, shall put to the European Parliament its proposed candidate for the Presidency of the Commission. This candidate shall be elected by the European Parliament by a majority of its members. If this candidate does not receive the required majority support, the European Council shall within one month put forward a new candidate, following the same procedure as before.

2.   Each Member State determined by the system of rotation shall establish a list of three persons, in which both genders shall be represented, whom it considers qualified to be a European Commissioner. By choosing one person from each of the proposed lists, the President-elect shall select the thirteen European Commissioners for their competence, European commitment, and guaranteed independence. The President and the persons so nominated for membership of the College, including the future Union Minister for Foreign Affairs, as well as the persons nominated as non-voting Commissioners, shall be submitted collectively to a vote of approval by the European Parliament. The Commission's term of office shall be five years.

3.   President of the Commission shall:

- lay down guidelines within which the Commission is to work;
- decide its internal organisation, ensuring that it acts consistently, efficiently and on a collegiate basis;
- appoint Vice-Presidents from among the members of the College.

A European Commissioner or Commissioner shall resign if the President so requests.

Article 27   THE UNION MINISTER FOR
FOREIGN AFFAIRS

1.   The European Council, acting by qualified majority, with the agreement of the President of the Commission, shall appoint the Union Minister for Foreign Affairs. He shall conduct the Union's common foreign and security policy. The European Council may end his tenure by the same procedure.

2.   The Union Minister for Foreign Affairs shall contribute by his proposals to the development of the common foreign policy, which he shall carry out as mandated by the Council of Ministers. The same shall apply to the common security and defence policy.

3.   The Union Minister for Foreign Affairs shall be one of the Vice-Presidents of the Commission. He shall be responsible there for handling external relations and for coordinating other aspects of the Union's external action. In exercising these responsibilities within the Commission, and only for these responsibilities, the Union Minister for Foreign Affairs shall be bound by Commission procedures.

Article 28   THE COURT OF JUSTICE

1.   The Court of Justice shall include the European Court of Justice, the High Court and specialised courts. It shall ensure respect for the law in the interpretation and application of the Constitution.

Member States shall provide rights of appeal sufficient to ensure effective legal protection in the field of Union law.

2.   The European Court of Justice shall consist of one judge from each Member State, and shall be assisted by Advocates-General.

The High Court shall include at least one judge per Member State: the number shall be fixed by the Statute of the Court of Justice.

The judges and the Advocates-General of the European Court of Justice and the judges of the High Court, chosen from persons whose independence is beyond doubt and who satisfy the conditions set out in Articles III-260 and III-261, shall be appointed by common accord of the governments of the Member States for a term of six years, renewable.

3.   The Court of Justice shall:

- rule on actions brought by a Member State, an Institution or a natural or legal person in accordance with the provisions of Part III;
- give preliminary rulings, at the request of Member State courts, on the interpretation of Union law or the validity of acts adopted by the Institutions;
- rule on the other cases provided for in the Constitution.

Chapter II   OTHER INSTITUTIONS AND BODIES

Article 29   THE EUROPEAN CENTRAL BANK

1.   The European Central Bank, together with the national central banks, shall constitute the European System of Central Banks. The European Central Bank, together with the national central banks of the Member States which have adopted the Union currency, the euro, shall conduct the monetary policy of the Union.

2.   The European System of Central Banks shall be governed by the decision-making bodies of the European Central Bank. The primary objective of the European System of Central Banks shall be to maintain price stability. Without

prejudice to the objective of price stability, it shall support general economic policies in the Union with a view to contributing to the achievement of the Union's objectives. It shall conduct other Central Bank tasks according to the provisions of Part III and the Statute of the European System of Central Banks and the European Central Bank.

3.   The European Central Bank is an Institution which has legal personality. It alone may authorise the issue of the euro. In the exercise of its powers and for its finances, it shall be independent. Union Institutions and bodies, and the governments of the Member States, shall undertake to respect this principle.

4.   The European Central Bank shall adopt such measures as are necessary to carry out its tasks in accordance with the provisions of Articles III-77 to III-83 and III-90, and with the conditions laid down in the Statute of the European System of Central Banks and the European Central Bank. In accordance with these same provisions, those Member States which have not adopted the euro, and their central banks, shall retain their powers in monetary matters.

5.   Within its areas of competence, the European Central Bank shall be consulted on all proposed Union acts, and all proposals for regulation at national level, and may give an opinion.

6.   The decision-making organs of the European Central Bank, their composition and operating methods are set out in Articles III-84 to III-87, as well as in the Statute of the European System of Central Banks and of the European Central Bank.

Article 30   THE COURT OF AUDITORS

1.   The Court of Auditors is the Institution which shall carry out the audit.

2.   It shall examine the accounts of all Union revenue and expenditure, and shall ensure good financial management.

3.   It shall consist of one national of each Member State. In the performance of their duties, its members shall be completely independent.

Article 31   THE UNION'S ADVISORY BODIES

1.   The European Parliament, the Council of Ministers and the Commission shall be assisted by a Committee of the Regions and an Economic and Social Committee, exercising advisory functions.

2.   The Committee of the Regions shall consist of representatives of regional and local bodies who either hold a regional or local authority electoral mandate or are politically accountable to an elected assembly.

3.   The Economic and Social Committee shall consist of representatives of organisations of employers, of the employed, and of others representative of civil society, notably in socio-economic, civic, professional and cultural areas.

4.   The members of the Committee of the Regions and the Economic and Social Committee must not be bound by any mandatory instructions. They shall be completely independent, in the performance of their duties, in the Union's general interest.

5.   Rules governing the composition of these Committees, the designation of their members, their powers and their operations, are set out in Articles III-292 to III-298. The rules governing their composition shall be reviewed at regular intervals by the Council of Ministers, on the basis of a Commission proposal, in the light of economic, social and demographic developments within the Union.

EXERCISE OF UNION COMPETENCE

Chapter I

COMMON PROVISIONS

THE LEGAL ACTS OF THE UNION

1.   In exercising the competences conferred on it in the Constitution, the Union shall use as legal instruments, in accordance with the provisions of Part III, European laws, European framework laws, European regulations, European decisions, recommendations and opinions.

A European law shall be a legislative act of general application. It shall be binding in its entirety and directly applicable in all Member States.

A European framework law shall be a legislative act binding, as to the result to be achieved, on the Member States to which it is addressed, but leaving the national authorities entirely free to choose the form and means of achieving that result.

A European regulation shall be a non-legislative act of general application for the implementation of legislative acts and of certain specific provisions of the Constitution. It may either be binding in its entirety and directly applicable in all Member States, or be binding, as regards the result to be achieved, on all Member States to which it is addressed, but leaving the national authorities entirely free to choose the form and means of achieving that result.

A European decision shall be a non-legislative act, binding in its entirety. A decision which specifies those to whom it is addressed shall be binding only on them.

Recommendations and opinions adopted by the Institutions shall have no binding force.

2.   When considering proposals for legislative acts, the European Parliament and the Council of Ministers shall refrain from adopting acts not provided for by this Article in the area in question.

Article 33   LEGISLATIVE ACTS

1.   European laws and European framework laws shall be adopted, on the basis of proposals from the Commission, jointly by the European Parliament and the Council of Ministers under the ordinary legislative procedure as set out in Article III-302. If the two Institutions cannot reach agreement on an act, it shall not be adopted.

In the cases specifically provided for in Article III-165, European laws and European framework laws may be adopted at the initiative of a group of Member States in accordance with Article III-302.

2.　　　　　In the specific cases provided for by the Constitution, European laws and European framework laws shall be adopted by the European Parliament with the participation of the Council of Ministers, or by the latter with the participation of the European Parliament, in accordance with special legislative procedures.

Article 34　　　NON-LEGISLATIVE ACTS

1.　　　　　The Council of Ministers and the Commission shall adopt European regulations or European decisions in the cases referred to in Articles 35 and 36 and in the cases specifically provided for in the Constitution. The European Council shall adopt European decisions in the cases specifically provided for in the Constitution. The European Central Bank shall adopt European regulations and European decisions when authorised to do so by the Constitution.

2.　　　　　The Council of Ministers and the Commission, and the European Central Bank when so authorised in the Constitution, adopt recommendations.

Article 35　　　DELEGATED REGULATIONS

1.　　　　　European laws and European framework laws may delegate to the Commission the power to enact delegated regulations to supplement or amend certain non-essential elements of the European law or framework law.

The objectives, content, scope and duration of the delegation shall be explicitly defined in the European laws and framework laws. A delegation may not cover the essential elements of an area. These shall be reserved for the European law or framework law.

2.   The conditions of application to which the delegation is subject shall be explicitly determined in the laws and framework laws. They may consist of the following possibilities:

> – the European Parliament or the Council of Ministers may decide to revoke the delegation;
> – the delegated regulation may enter into force only if no objection has been expressed by the European Parliament or the Council of Ministers within a period set by the European law or framework law.

For the purposes of the preceding paragraph, the European Parliament shall act by a majority of its members, and the Council of Ministers by a qualified majority.

Article 36   IMPLEMENTING ACTS

1.   Member States shall adopt all measures of national law necessary to implement legally binding Union acts.

2.   Where uniform conditions for implementing binding Union acts are needed, those acts may confer implementing powers on the Commission, or, in specific cases duly justified and in the cases provided for in Article 39, on the Council of Ministers.

3.   The European laws shall lay down in advance rules and general principles for the mechanisms for control by Member States of Union implementing acts.

4.   Union implementing acts shall take the form of European implementing regulations or European implementing decisions.

Article 37   PRINCIPLES COMMON TO THE
                   UNION'S LEGAL ACTS

1.   Unless the Constitution contains a specific stipulation, the Institutions shall decide, in compliance with the procedures applicable, the type of act to be adopted in each case, in accordance with the principle of proportionality set out in Article 9.

2.   European laws, European framework laws, European regulations and European decisions shall state the reasons on which they are based and shall refer to any proposals or opinions required by this Constitution.

Article 38   PUBLICATION AND ENTRY INTO FORCE

1.   European laws and framework laws adopted under the ordinary legislative procedure shall be signed by the President of the European Parliament and by the President of the Council of Ministers. In other cases they shall be signed by the President of the European Parliament or by the President of the Council of Ministers. European laws and European framework laws shall be published in the Official Journal of the European Union and shall enter into force on the date specified in them or, in the absence of such a stated date, on the twentieth day following their publication.

2.   European regulations and European decisions which do not specify to whom they are addressed or which are addressed to all Member States shall be signed by the President of the Institution which adopts them, shall be published in the Official Journal of the European Union and shall enter into force on the date specified in them or, in the absence of such a stated date, on the twentieth day following their publication.

3.   Other decisions shall be notified to those to whom they are addressed and shall take effect upon such notification.

Chapter II   SPECIFIC PROVISIONS

Article 39   SPECIFIC PROVISIONS FOR
IMPLEMENTING COMMON FOREIGN
AND SECURITY POLICY

1.   The European Union shall conduct a common foreign and security policy, based on the development of mutual political solidarity among Member States, the identification of questions of general interest and the achievement of an ever-increasing degree of convergence of Member States' actions.

2.   The European Council shall identify the Union's strategic interests and determine the objectives of its common foreign and security policy. The Council of Ministers shall frame this policy within the framework of the strategic guidelines established by the European Council and in accordance with the arrangements in Part III.

3.   The European Council and the Council of Ministers shall adopt the necessary European decisions.

4.   The common foreign and security policy shall be put into effect by the Union Minister for Foreign Affairs and by the Member States, using national and Union resources.

5.	Member States shall consult one another within the European Council and the Council of Ministers on any foreign and security policy issue which is of general interest in order to determine a common approach. Before undertaking any action on the international scene or any commitment which could affect the Union's interests, each Member State shall consult the others within the European Council or the Council of Ministers. Member States shall ensure, through the convergence of their actions, that the Union is able to assert its interests and values on the international scene. Member States shall show mutual solidarity.

6.	The European Parliament shall be regularly consulted on the main aspects and basic choices of the common foreign and security policy, and shall be kept informed of how it evolves.

7.	European decisions relating to the common foreign and security policy shall be adopted by the European Council and the Council of Ministers unanimously, except in the cases referred to in Part III. The European Council and the Council of Ministers shall act on a proposal from a Member State, from the Union Minister for Foreign Affairs or from that Minister with the Commission's support. European laws and European framework laws are excluded.

8.	The European Council may unanimously decide that the Council of Ministers should act by qualified majority in cases other than those referred to in Part III.

Article 40   SPECIFIC PROVISIONS FOR
IMPLEMENTING THE COMMON
SECURITY AND DEFENCE POLICY

1.   The common security and defence policy shall be an integral part of the common foreign and security policy. It shall provide the Union with an operational capacity drawing on assets civil and military. The Union may use them on missions outside the Union for peace-keeping, conflict prevention and strengthening international security in accordance with the principles of the United Nations Charter. The performance of these tasks shall be undertaken using capabilities provided by the Member States.

2.   The common security and defence policy shall include the progressive framing of a common Union defence policy. This will lead to a common defence, when the European Council, acting unanimously, so decides. It shall in that case recommend to the Member States the adoption of such a decision in accordance with their respective constitutional requirements.

The policy of the Union in accordance with this Article shall not prejudice the specific character of the security and defence policy of certain Member States and shall respect the obligations of certain Member States, which see their common defence realised in the North Atlantic Treaty Organisation, under the North Atlantic Treaty, and be compatible with the common security and defence policy established within that framework.

3.   Member States shall make civilian and military capabilities available to the Union for the implementation of the common security and defence policy, to contribute to the objectives defined by the Council of Ministers. Those Member States which together establish multinational forces may also make those forces available to the common security and defence policy.

Member States shall undertake progressively to improve their military capabilities. A European Armaments, Research and Military Capabilities Agency shall be established to identify operational requirements, to promote measures to satisfy those requirements, to contribute to identifying and, where appropriate, implementing any measure needed to strengthen the industrial and technological base of the defence sector, to participate in defining a European capabilities and armaments policy, and to assist the Council of Ministers in evaluating the improvement of military capabilities.

4.   European decisions on the implementation of the common security and defence policy, including those initiating a mission as referred to in this Article, shall be adopted by the Council of Ministers acting unanimously on a proposal from the Union Minister for Foreign Affairs or from a Member State. The Union Minister for Foreign Affairs may propose the use of both national resources and Union instruments, together with the Commission where appropriate.

5.   The Council of Ministers may entrust the execution of a task, within the Union framework, to a group of

Member States in order to maintain the Union's values and serve its interests. The execution of such a task shall be governed by Article III-211.

6.   Those Member States whose military capabilities fulfil higher criteria and which have made more binding commitments to one another in this area with a view to the most demanding missions shall establish structured cooperation within the Union framework. Such cooperation shall be governed by the provisions of Article III-213.

7.   Until such time as the European Council has acted in accordance with paragraph 2 of this Article, closer cooperation shall be established, in the Union framework, as regards mutual defence. Under this cooperation, if one of the Member States participating in such cooperation is the victim of armed aggression on its territory, the other participating States shall give it aid and assistance by all the means in their power, military or other, in accordance with Article 51 of the United Nations Charter. In the execution of closer cooperation on mutual defence, the participating Member States shall work in close cooperation with the North Atlantic Treaty Organisation. The detailed arrangements for participation in this cooperation and its operation, and the relevant decision-making procedures, are set out in Article III-214.

8.   The European Parliament shall be regularly consulted on the main aspects and basic choices of the common security and defence policy, and shall be kept informed of how it evolves.

Article 41   SPECIFIC PROVISIONS FOR
IMPLEMENTING THE AREA OF
FREEDOM, SECURITY AND JUSTICE

1.   The Union shall constitute an area of freedom,
security and justice:

- by adopting European laws and framework laws intended, where necessary, to approximate national laws in the areas listed in Part III;
- by promoting mutual confidence between the competent authorities of the Member States, in particular on the basis of mutual recognition of judicial and extrajudicial decisions;
- by operational cooperation between the competent authorities of the Member States, including the police, customs and other services specialising in the prevention and detection of criminal offences.

2.   Within the area of freedom, security and justice, national parliaments may participate in the evaluation mechanisms foreseen in Article III-161, and shall be involved in the political monitoring of Europol and the evaluation of Eurojust's activities in accordance with Articles III-177 and III-174.

3.　　　　In the field of police and judicial cooperation in criminal matters, Member States shall have a right of initiative in accordance with Article III-165 of the Constitution.

Article 42　　　SOLIDARITY CLAUSE

1.　　　　The Union and its Member States shall act jointly in a spirit of solidarity if a Member State is the victim of terrorist attack or natural or man-made disaster. The Union shall mobilise all the instruments at its disposal, including the military resources made available by the Member States, to:

> *(a)* – prevent the terrorist threat in the territory of the Member States;
> – protect democratic institutions and the civilian population from any terrorist attack;
> – assist a Member State in its territory at the request of its political authorities in the event of a terrorist attack;
> *(b)* – assist a Member State in its territory at the request of its political authorities in the event of a disaster.

2.　　　　The detailed arrangements for implementing this provision are at Article III-231.

Chapter III   ENHANCED COOPERATION

Article 43   ENHANCED COOPERATION

1.   Member States which wish to establish enhanced cooperation between themselves within the framework of the Union's non-exclusive competences may make use of its Institutions and exercise those competences by applying the relevant provisions of the Constitution, subject to the limits and in accordance with the procedures laid down in this Article and in Articles III-321 to III-328.

Enhanced cooperation shall aim to further the objectives of the Union, protect its interests and reinforce its integration process. Such cooperation shall be open to all Member States when it is being established and at any time, in accordance with Article III-324.

2.   Authorisation to proceed with enhanced cooperation shall be granted by the Council of Ministers as a last resort, when it has been established within the Council of Ministers that the objectives of such cooperation cannot be attained within a reasonable period by the Union as a whole, and provided that it brings together at least one third of the Member States. The Council of Ministers shall act in accordance with the procedure laid down in Article III-325.

3.   Only members of the Council of Ministers representing the States participating in enhanced cooperation shall take part in the adoption of acts. All Member States may, however, take part in the deliberations of the Council of Ministers.

Unanimity shall be constituted by the votes of the representatives of the participating States only. A qualified majority shall be defined as a majority of the votes of the representatives of the participating States, representing at least three fifths of the population of those States. Where the Constitution does not require the Council of Ministers to act on the basis of a Commission proposal, or where the Council of Ministers is not acting upon initiative of the Minister for Foreign Affairs, the required qualified majority shall be defined as a majority of two thirds of the participating States, representing at least three fifths of the population of those States.

4.   Acts adopted in the framework of enhanced cooperation shall bind only participating States. They shall not be regarded as an acquis which has to be accepted by candidates for accession to the Union.

| *Title VI* | # THE DEMOCRATIC LIFE OF THE UNION |

THE DEMOCRATIC LIFE OF THE UNION

Article 44 **THE PRINCIPLE OF DEMOCRATIC EQUALITY**

In all its activities, the Union shall observe the principle of the equality of citizens. All shall receive equal attention from the Union's Institutions.

Article 45 **THE PRINCIPLE OF REPRESENTATIVE DEMOCRACY**

1. The working of the Union shall be founded on the principle of representative democracy.

2. Citizens are directly represented at Union level in the European Parliament. Member States are represented in the European Council and in the Council of Ministers by their governments, themselves accountable to national parliaments, elected by their citizens.

3. Every citizen shall have the right to participate in the democratic life of the Union. Decisions shall be taken as openly as possible and as closely as possible to the citizen.

4.   Political parties at European level contribute to forming European political awareness and to expressing the will of Union citizens.

Article 46   THE PRINCIPLE OF
                 PARTICIPATORY DEMOCRACY

1.   The Union Institutions shall, by appropriate means, give citizens and representative associations the opportunity to make known and publicly exchange their views on all areas of Union action.

2.   The Union Institutions shall maintain an open, transparent and regular dialogue with representative associations and civil society.

3.   The Commission shall carry out broad consultations with parties concerned in order to ensure that the Union's actions are coherent and transparent.

4.   No less than one million citizens coming from a significant number of Member States may invite the Commission to submit any appropriate proposal on matters where citizens consider that a legal act of the Union is required for the purpose of implementing this Constitution. A European law shall determine the provisions for the specific procedures and conditions required for such a citizens' initiative.

Article 47   THE SOCIAL PARTNERS AND
             AUTONOMOUS SOCIAL DIALOGUE

The European Union recognises and promotes the role of the
social partners at Union level, taking into account the diversity of national systems; it shall facilitate dialogue between the
social partners, respecting their autonomy.

Article 48   THE EUROPEAN OMBUDSMAN

A European Ombudsman appointed by the European Parliament shall receive, investigate and report on complaints
about maladministration within the Union Institutions, bodies or agencies. The European Ombudsman shall be completely independent in the performance of his duties.

Article 49   TRANSPARENCY OF THE PROCEEDINGS
             OF UNION INSTITUTIONS

1.   In order to promote good governance and
ensure the participation of civil society, the Union Institutions, bodies and agencies shall conduct their work as openly
as possible.

2.   The European Parliament shall meet in public,
as shall the Council of Ministers when examining and adopting a legislative proposal.

3. Any citizen of the Union, and any natural or legal person residing or having its registered office in a Member State shall have a right of access to documents of the Union Institutions, bodies and agencies in whatever form they are produced, in accordance with the conditions laid down in Part III.

4. A European law shall lay down the general principles and limits which, on grounds of public or private interest, govern the right of access to such documents.

5. Each Institution, body or agency referred to in paragraph 3 shall determine in its own rules of procedure specific provisions regarding access to its documents, in accordance with the European law referred to in paragraph 4.

Article 50 PROTECTION OF PERSONAL DATA

1. Everyone has the right to the protection of personal data concerning him or her.

2. A European law shall lay down the rules relating to the protection of individuals with regard to the processing of personal data by Union Institutions, bodies and agencies, and by the Member States when carrying out activities which come under the scope of Union law, and the rules relating to the free movement of such data. Compliance with these rules shall be subject to the control of an independent authority.

Article 51   STATUS OF CHURCHES AND
                 NON-CONFESSIONAL ORGANISATIONS

1.   The Union respects and does not prejudice the
status under national law of churches and religious associations or communities in the Member States.

2.   The Union equally respects the status of philosophical and non-confessional organisations.

3.   Recognising their identity and their specific contribution, the Union shall maintain an open, transparent and regular dialogue with these churches and organisations.

Title VII　　# THE UNION'S FINANCES

Article 52　　BUDGETARY AND FINANCIAL
　　　　　　　PRINCIPLES

1.　　　　All items of Union revenue and expenditure shall be included in estimates drawn up for each financial year and shall be shown in the budget, in accordance with the provisions of Part III.

2.　　　　The revenue and expenditure shown in the budget shall be in balance.

3.　　　　The expenditure shown in the budget shall be authorised for the annual budgetary period in accordance with the European law referred to in Article III-318.

4.　　　　The implementation of expenditure shown in the budget shall require the prior adoption of a binding legal act providing a legal basis for Union action and for the implementation of the expenditure in accordance with the European law referred to in Article III-318. This act must take the form of a European law, a European framework law, a European regulation or a European decision.

5.　　　　With a view to maintaining budgetary discipline, the Union shall not adopt any act which is likely to have appreciable implications for the budget without providing an assurance that the proposal or measure in question is capable of being financed within the limit of the Union's own resources and the multiannual financial framework referred to in Article 54.

6.   The Union's budget shall be implemented in accordance with the principle of sound financial management. Member States shall cooperate with the Union to ensure that the appropriations entered in the budget are used in accordance with the principles of sound financial management.

7.   The Union and the Member States shall counter fraud and any other illegal activities affecting the financial interests of the Union in accordance with the provisions of Article III-321.

Article 53   THE UNION'S RESOURCES

1.   The Union shall provide itself with the means necessary to attain its objectives and carry through its policies.

2.   Without prejudice to other revenue, the Union's budget shall be financed wholly from its own resources.

3.   A European law of the Council of Ministers shall lay down the limit of the Union's resources and may

establish new categories of resources or abolish an existing category. That law shall not enter into force until it is approved by the Member States in accordance with their respective constitutional requirements. The Council of Ministers shall act unanimously after consulting the European Parliament.

4.   A European law of the Council shall lay down the modalities relating to the Union's resources. The Council of Ministers shall act after obtaining the consent of the European Parliament.

Article 54	THE MULTIANNUAL FINANCIAL FRAMEWORK

1.   The multiannual financial framework shall ensure that Union expenditure develops in an orderly manner and within the own resources limits. It shall determine the amounts of the annual ceilings for commitment appropriations by category of expenditure in accordance with the provisions of Article III-308.

2.   A European law of the Council of Ministers shall lay down the multiannual financial framework. The Council of Ministers shall act after obtaining the consent of the European Parliament, which shall be given by a majority of its component members.

3.   The annual budget of the Union shall comply with the multiannual financial framework.

4.   The Council of Ministers shall act unanimously when adopting the first multiannual financial framework following the entry into force of the Constitution.

Article 55   THE UNION'S BUDGET

The European Parliament and the Council of Ministers shall, on a proposal from the Commission and in accordance with the arrangements laid down in Article III-310, adopt the European law determining the Union's annual budget.

THE UNION AND ITS IMMEDIATE ENVIRONMENT

Article 56   THE UNION AND ITS
                 IMMEDIATE ENVIRONMENT

1.   The Union shall develop a special relationship with neighbouring States, aiming to establish an area of prosperity and good neighbourliness, founded on the values of the Union and characterised by close and peaceful relations based on cooperation.

2.   For this purpose, the Union may conclude and implement specific agreements with the countries concerned in accordance with Article III-227. These agreements may contain reciprocal rights and obligations as well as the possibility of undertaking activities jointly. Their implementation shall be the subject of periodic consultation.

UNION MEMBERSHIP

Article 57 ## CONDITIONS OF ELIGIBILITY AND PROCEDURE FOR ACCESSION TO THE UNION

1.   The Union shall be open to all European States which respect the values referred to in Article 2, and are committed to promoting them together.

2.   Any European State which wishes to become a member of the Union may address its application to the Council of Ministers. The European Parliament and the Member States' national Parliaments shall be notified of this application. The Council of Ministers shall act unanimously after consulting the Commission and after obtaining the consent of the European Parliament. The conditions and arrangements for admission shall be the subject of an agreement between the Member States and the candidate State. That agreement shall be subject to ratification by each contracting State, in accordance with its respective constitutional requirements.

Article 58 ## SUSPENSION OF UNION MEMBERSHIP RIGHTS

1.   On a reasoned proposal by one third of the Member States, by the European Parliament or by the Com-

mission, the Council of Ministers, acting by a majority of four fifths of its members after obtaining the consent of the European Parliament, may adopt a European decision determining that there is a clear risk of a serious breach by a Member State of the values mentioned in Article 2. Before making such a determination, the Council of Ministers shall hear the Member State in question and, acting in accordance with the same procedure, may address recommendations to that State.

The Council of Ministers shall regularly verify that the grounds on which such a determination was made continue to apply.

2.   The European Council, acting by unanimity on a proposal by one third of the Member States or by the Commission and after obtaining the consent of the European Parliament, may adopt a European decision determining the existence of a serious and persistent breach by a Member State of the values mentioned in Article 2, after inviting the Member State in question to submit its observations.

3.   Where a determination under paragraph 2 has been made, the Council of Ministers, acting by a qualified majority, may adopt a European decision suspending certain of the rights deriving from the application of the Constitution to the Member State in question, including the voting rights of that Member State in the Council of Ministers. In so doing, the Council of Ministers shall take into account the possible consequences of such a suspension on the rights and obligations of natural and legal persons.

That Member State shall in any case continue to be bound by its obligations under the Constitution.

4.   The Council of Ministers, acting by a qualified majority, may subsequently adopt a European decision varying or revoking measures taken under paragraph 3 in response to changes in the situation which led to their being imposed.

5.   For the purposes of this Article, the Council of Ministers shall act without taking into account the vote of the Member State in question. Abstentions by members present in person or represented shall not prevent the adoption of decisions referred to in paragraph 2.

This paragraph shall also apply in the event of voting rights being suspended pursuant to paragraph 3.

6.   For the purposes of paragraphs 1 and 2, the European Parliament shall act by a two-thirds majority of the votes cast, representing the majority of its Members.

Article 59   VOLUNTARY WITHDRAWAL FROM THE UNION

1.   Any Member State may decide to withdraw from the European Union in accordance with its own constitutional requirements.

2. A Member State which decides to withdraw shall notify the European Council of its intention; the European Council shall examine that notification. In the light of the guidelines provided by the European Council, the Union shall negotiate and conclude an agreement with that State, setting out the arrangements for its withdrawal, taking account of the framework for its future relationship with the Union. That agreement shall be concluded on behalf of the Union by the Council of Ministers, acting by a qualified majority, after obtaining the consent of the European Parliament.

The representative of the withdrawing Member State shall not participate in Council of Ministers or European Council discussions or decisions concerning it.

3. This Constitution shall cease to apply to the State in question from the date of entry into force of the withdrawal agreement or, failing that, two years after the notification referred to in paragraph 2, unless the European Council, in agreement with the Member State concerned, decides to extend this period.

4. If a State which has withdrawn from the Union asks to re-join, that request shall be subject to the procedure referred to in Article 57.

PART II

THE CHARTER OF FUNDAMENTAL RIGHTS OF THE UNION

PREAMBLE

The peoples of Europe, in creating an ever closer union among them, are resolved to share a peaceful future based on common values.

Conscious of its spiritual and moral heritage, the Union is founded on the indivisible, universal values of human dignity, freedom, equality and solidarity; it is based on the principles of democracy and the rule of law. It places the individual at the heart of its activities, by establishing the citizenship of the Union and by creating an area of freedom, security and justice.

The Union contributes to the preservation and to the development of these common values while respecting the diversity of the cultures and traditions of the peoples of Europe as well as the national identities of the Member States and the organisation of their public authorities at national, regional and local levels; it seeks to promote balanced and sustainable development and ensures free movement of persons, goods, services and capital, and the freedom of establishment.

To this end, it is necessary to strengthen the protection of fundamental rights in the light of changes in society, social progress and scientific and technological developments by making those rights more visible in a Charter.

This Charter reaffirms, with due regard for the powers and tasks of the Union and the principle of subsidiarity, the rights as they result, in particular, from the constitutional traditions and international obligations common to the Member States, the European Convention for the Protection of Human Rights and Fundamental Freedoms, the Social Charters adopted by the Union and by the Council of Europe and the case law of the Court of Justice of the European Union and of the European Court of Human Rights. In this context the Charter will be interpreted by the courts of the Union and the Member States with due regard to the explanations prepared at the instigation of the Praesidium of the Convention which drafted the Charter.

Enjoyment of these rights entails responsibilities and duties with regard to other persons, to the human community and to future generations.

The Union therefore recognises the rights, freedoms and principles set out hereafter.

Title I   # DIGNITY

Article II-1   ## HUMAN DIGNITY

Human dignity is inviolable. It must be respected and protected.

Article II-2   ## RIGHT TO LIFE

1.   Everyone has the right to life.

2.   No one shall be condemned to the death penalty, or executed.

Article II-3   ## RIGHT TO THE INTEGRITY OF THE PERSON

1.   Everyone has the right to respect for his or her physical and mental integrity.

2.   In the fields of medicine and biology, the following must be respected in particular:

   (a) the free and informed consent of the person concerned, according to the procedures laid down by law,

(b) the prohibition of eugenic practices, in particular those aiming at the selection of persons,

(c) the prohibition on making the human body and its parts as such a source of financial gain,

(d) the prohibition of the reproductive cloning of human beings.

Article II-4   PROHIBITION OF TORTURE AND
                  INHUMAN OR DEGRADING
                  TREATMENT OR PUNISHMENT

No one shall be subjected to torture or to inhuman or degrading treatment or punishment.

Article II-5   PROHIBITION OF SLAVERY AND
                  FORCED LABOUR

1.   No one shall be held in slavery or servitude.

2.   No one shall be required to perform forced or compulsory labour.

3.   Trafficking in human beings is prohibited.

Title II   # FREEDOMS

Article II-6   ## RIGHT TO LIBERTY AND SECURITY

Everyone has the right to liberty and security of person.

Article II-7   ## RESPECT FOR PRIVATE AND FAMILY LIFE

Everyone has the right to respect for his or her private and family life, home and communications.

Article II-8   ## PROTECTION OF PERSONAL DATA

1.   Everyone has the right to the protection of personal data concerning him or her.

2.   Such data must be processed fairly for specified purposes and on the basis of the consent of the person concerned or some other legitimate basis laid down by law. Everyone has the right of access to data which has been collected concerning him or her, and the right to have it rectified.

3.   Compliance with these rules shall be subject to control by an independent authority.

Article II-9   RIGHT TO MARRY AND
RIGHT TO FOUND A FAMILY

The right to marry and the right to found a family shall be guaranteed in accordance with the national laws governing the exercise of these rights.

Article II-10   FREEDOM OF THOUGHT,
CONSCIENCE AND RELIGION

1.   Everyone has the right to freedom of thought, conscience and religion. This right includes freedom to change religion or belief and freedom, either alone or in community with others and in public or in private, to manifest religion or belief, in worship, teaching, practice and observance.

2.   The right to conscientious objection is recognised, in accordance with the national laws governing the exercise of this right.

Article II-11   FREEDOM OF EXPRESSION AND
INFORMATION

1.   Everyone has the right to freedom of expression. This right shall include freedom to hold opinions and to receive and impart information and ideas without interference by public authority and regardless of frontiers.

2.   The freedom and pluralism of the media shall be respected.

Article II-12 FREEDOM OF ASSEMBLY AND OF ASSOCIATION

1.   Everyone has the right to freedom of peaceful assembly and to freedom of association at all levels, in particular in political, trade union and civic matters, which implies the right of everyone to form and to join trade unions for the protection of his or her interests.

2.   Political parties at Union level contribute to expressing the political will of the citizens of the Union.

Article II-13 FREEDOM OF THE ARTS AND SCIENCES

The arts and scientific research shall be free of constraint. Academic freedom shall be respected.

Article II-14 RIGHT TO EDUCATION

1.   Everyone has the right to education and to have access to vocational and continuing training.

2.   This right includes the possibility to receive free compulsory education.

3.   The freedom to found educational establishments with due respect for democratic principles and the right of parents to ensure the education and teaching of their children in conformity with their religious, philosophical and pedagogical convictions shall be respected, in accordance with the national laws governing the exercise of such freedom and right.

Article II-15 FREEDOM TO CHOOSE AN OCCUPATION AND RIGHT TO ENGAGE IN WORK

1.   Everyone has the right to engage in work and to pursue a freely chosen or accepted occupation.

2.   Every citizen of the Union has the freedom to seek employment, to work, to exercise the right of establishment and to provide services in any Member State.

3.   Nationals of third countries who are authorised to work in the territories of the Member States are entitled to working conditions equivalent to those of citizens of the Union.

Article II-16   FREEDOM TO CONDUCT A BUSINESS

The freedom to conduct a business in accordance with Union law and national laws and practices is recognised.

Article II-17   RIGHT TO PROPERTY

1.   Everyone has the right to own, use, dispose of and bequeath his or her lawfully acquired possessions. No one may be deprived of his or her possessions, except in the public interest and in the cases and under the conditions provided for by law, subject to fair compensation being paid in good time for their loss. The use of property may be regulated by law insofar as is necessary for the general interest.

2.   Intellectual property shall be protected.

Article II-18   RIGHT TO ASYLUM

The right to asylum shall be guaranteed with due respect for the rules of the Geneva Convention of 28 July 1951 and the Protocol of 31 January 1967 relating to the status of refugees and in accordance with the Constitution.

Article II-19 PROTECTION IN THE EVENT OF
REMOVAL, EXPULSION OR
EXTRADITION

1. Collective expulsions are prohibited.

2. No one may be removed, expelled or extradited
to a State where there is a serious risk that he or she would be
subjected to the death penalty, torture or other inhuman or
degrading treatment or punishment.

Title III   # EQUALITY

Article II-20   ## EQUALITY BEFORE THE LAW

Everyone is equal before the law.

Article II-21   ## NON-DISCRIMINATION

1.   Any discrimination based on any ground such as sex, race, colour, ethnic or social origin, genetic features, language, religion or belief, political or any other opinion, membership of a national minority, property, birth, disability, age or sexual orientation shall be prohibited.

2.   Within the scope of application of the Constitution and without prejudice to any of its specific provisions, any discrimination on grounds of nationality shall be prohibited.

Article II-22   ## CULTURAL, RELIGIOUS AND LINGUISTIC DIVERSITY

The Union shall respect cultural, religious and linguistic diversity.

Article II-23 EQUALITY BETWEEN
MEN AND WOMEN

Equality between men and women must be ensured in all areas, including employment, work and pay.

The principle of equality shall not prevent the maintenance or adoption of measures providing for specific advantages in favour of the under-represented sex.

Article II-24 THE RIGHTS OF THE CHILD

1. Children shall have the right to such protection and care as is necessary for their well-being. They may express their views freely. Such views shall be taken into consideration on matters which concern them in accordance with their age and maturity.

2. In all actions relating to children, whether taken by public authorities or private Institutions, the child's best interests must be a primary consideration.

3. Every child shall have the right to maintain on a regular basis a personal relationship and direct contact with both his or her parents, unless that is contrary to his or her interests.

Article II-25   THE RIGHTS OF THE ELDERLY

The Union recognises and respects the rights of the elderly to lead a life of dignity and independence and to participate in social and cultural life.

Article II-26   INTEGRATION OF
               PERSONS WITH DISABILITIES

The Union recognises and respects the right of persons with disabilities to benefit from measures designed to ensure their independence, social and occupational integration and participation in the life of the community.

Title IV # SOLIDARITY

Article II-27 ## WORKERS' RIGHT TO INFORMATION AND CONSULTATION WITHIN THE UNDERTAKING

Workers or their representatives must, at the appropriate levels, be guaranteed information and consultation in good time in the cases and under the conditions provided for by Union law and national laws and practices.

Article II-28 ## RIGHT OF COLLECTIVE BARGAINING AND ACTION

Workers and employers, or their respective organisations, have, in accordance with Union law and national laws and practices, the right to negotiate and conclude collective agreements at the appropriate levels and, in cases of conflicts of interest, to take collective action to defend their interests, including strike action.

Article II-29 ## RIGHT OF ACCESS TO PLACEMENT SERVICES

Everyone has the right of access to a free placement service.

Article II-30   PROTECTION IN THE EVENT OF UNJUSTIFIED DISMISSAL

Every worker has the right to protection against unjustified dismissal, in accordance with Union law and national laws and practices.

Article II-31   FAIR AND JUST WORKING CONDITIONS

1.   Every worker has the right to working conditions which respect his or her health, safety and dignity.

2.   Every worker has the right to limitation of maximum working hours, to daily and weekly rest periods and to an annual period of paid leave.

Article II-32   PROHIBITION OF CHILD LABOUR AND PROTECTION OF YOUNG PEOPLE AT WORK

The employment of children is prohibited. The minimum age of admission to employment may not be lower than the minimum school-leaving age, without prejudice to such rules as may be more favourable to young people and except for limited derogations.

Young people admitted to work must have working conditions appropriate to their age and be protected against economic exploitation and any work likely to harm their safety, health or physical, mental, moral or social development or to interfere with their education.

Article II-33 FAMILY AND PROFESSIONAL LIFE

1. The family shall enjoy legal, economic and social protection.

2. To reconcile family and professional life, everyone shall have the right to protection from dismissal for a reason connected with maternity and the right to paid maternity leave and to parental leave following the birth or adoption of a child.

Article II-34 SOCIAL SECURITY AND SOCIAL ASSISTANCE

1. The Union recognises and respects the entitlement to social security benefits and social services providing protection in cases such as maternity, illness, industrial accidents, dependency or old age, and in the case of loss of employment, in accordance with the rules laid down by Union law and national laws and practices.

2.   Everyone residing and moving legally within the European Union is entitled to social security benefits and social advantages in accordance with Union law and national laws and practices.

3.   In order to combat social exclusion and poverty, the Union recognises and respects the right to social and housing assistance so as to ensure a decent existence for all those who lack sufficient resources, in accordance with the rules laid down by Union law and national laws and practices.

Article II-35   HEALTH CARE

Everyone has the right of access to preventive health care and the right to benefit from medical treatment under the conditions established by national laws and practices. A high level of human health protection shall be ensured in the definition and implementation of all Union policies and activities.

Article II-36   ACCESS TO SERVICES OF
             GENERAL ECONOMIC INTEREST

The Union recognises and respects access to services of general economic interest as provided for in national laws and practices, in accordance with the Constitution, in order to promote the social and territorial cohesion of the Union.

Article II-37   ENVIRONMENTAL PROTECTION

A high level of environmental protection and the improvement of the quality of the environment must be integrated
into the policies of the Union and ensured in accordance with
the principle of sustainable development.

Article II-38   CONSUMER PROTECTION

Union policies shall ensure a high level of consumer protection.

Title V　　　**CITIZENS' RIGHTS**

Article II-39　**RIGHT TO VOTE AND TO STAND AS A CANDIDATE AT ELECTIONS TO THE EUROPEAN PARLIAMENT**

1.　　　　Every citizen of the Union has the right to vote and to stand as a candidate at elections to the European Parliament in the Member State in which he or she resides, under the same conditions as nationals of that State.

2.　　　　Members of the European Parliament shall be elected by direct universal suffrage in a free and secret ballot.

Article II-40　**RIGHT TO VOTE AND TO STAND AS A CANDIDATE AT MUNICIPAL ELECTIONS**

Every citizen of the Union has the right to vote and to stand as a candidate at municipal elections in the Member State in which he or she resides under the same conditions as nationals of that State.

Article II-41　**RIGHT TO GOOD ADMINISTRATION**

1.　　　　Every person has the right to have his or her affairs handled impartially, fairly and within a reasonable time by the Institutions, bodies and agencies of the Union.

2.   This right includes:

   (*a*) the right of every person to be heard, before any individual measure which would affect him or her adversely is taken;
   (*b*) the right of every person to have access to his or her file, while respecting the legitimate interests of confidentiality and of professional and business secrecy;
   (*c*) the obligation of the administration to give reasons for its decisions.

3.   Every person has the right to have the Union make good any damage caused by its Institutions or by its servants in the performance of their duties, in accordance with the general principles common to the laws of the Member States.

4.   Every person may write to the Institutions of the Union in one of the languages of the Constitution and must have an answer in the same language.

Article II-42   RIGHT OF ACCESS TO DOCUMENTS

Any citizen of the Union, and any natural or legal person residing or having its registered office in a Member State, has a right of access to documents of the Institutions, bodies and agencies of the Union, in whatever form they are produced.

Article II-43 EUROPEAN OMBUDSMAN

Any citizen of the Union and any natural or legal person residing or having its registered office in a Member State has the right to refer to the European Ombudsman cases of maladministration in the activities of the Institutions, bodies or agencies of the Union, with the exception of the European Court of Justice and the High Court acting in their judicial role.

Article II-44 RIGHT TO PETITION

Any citizen of the Union and any natural or legal person residing or having its registered office in a Member State has the right to petition the European Parliament.

Article II-45 FREEDOM OF MOVEMENT AND OF RESIDENCE

1. Every citizen of the Union has the right to move and reside freely within the territory of the Member States.

2. Freedom of movement and residence may be granted, in accordance with the Constitution, to nationals of third countries legally resident in the territory of a Member State.

Article II-46 DIPLOMATIC AND CONSULAR
PROTECTION

Every citizen of the Union shall, in the territory of a third country in which the Member State of which he or she is a national is not represented, be entitled to protection by the diplomatic or consular authorities of any Member State, on the same conditions as the nationals of that Member State.

Title VI # JUSTICE

Article II-47 ## RIGHT TO AN EFFECTIVE REMEDY AND TO A FAIR TRIAL

Everyone whose rights and freedoms guaranteed by the law of the Union are violated has the right to an effective remedy before a tribunal in compliance with the conditions laid down in this Article.

Everyone is entitled to a fair and public hearing within a reasonable time by an independent and impartial tribunal previously established by law. Everyone shall have the possibility of being advised, defended and represented.

Legal aid shall be made available to those who lack sufficient resources insofar as such aid is necessary to ensure effective access to justice.

Article II-48 ## PRESUMPTION OF INNOCENCE AND RIGHT OF DEFENCE

1. Everyone who has been charged shall be presumed innocent until proved guilty according to law.

2. Respect for the rights of the defence of anyone who has been charged shall be guaranteed.

Article II-49   PRINCIPLES OF LEGALITY AND
PROPORTIONALITY OF CRIMINAL
OFFENCES AND PENALTIES

1.   No one shall be held guilty of any criminal offence on account of any act or omission which did not constitute a criminal offence under national law or international law at the time when it was committed. Nor shall a heavier penalty be imposed than that which was applicable at the time the criminal offence was committed. If, subsequent to the commission of a criminal offence, the law provides for a lighter penalty, that penalty shall be applicable.

2.   This Article shall not prejudice the trial and punishment of any person for any act or omission which, at the time when it was committed, was criminal according to the general principles recognised by the community of nations.

3.   The severity of penalties must not be disproportionate to the criminal offence.

Article II-50   RIGHT NOT TO BE TRIED OR
PUNISHED TWICE IN CRIMINAL
PROCEEDINGS FOR THE SAME
CRIMINAL OFFENCE

No one shall be liable to be tried or punished again in criminal proceedings for an offence for which he or she has already been finally acquitted or convicted within the Union in accordance with the law.

GENERAL PROVISIONS GOVERNING THE INTERPRETATION AND APPLICATION OF THE CHARTER

Article II-51   FIELD OF APPLICATION

1.   The provisions of this Charter are addressed to the Institutions, bodies and agencies of the Union with due regard for the principle of subsidiarity and to the Member States only when they are implementing Union law. They shall therefore respect the rights, observe the principles and promote the application thereof in accordance with their respective powers and respecting the limits of the powers of the Union as conferred on it in the other Parts of the Constitution.

2.   This Charter does not extend the field of application of Union law beyond the powers of the Union or establish any new power or task for the Union, or modify powers and tasks defined in the other Parts of the Constitution.

Article II-52   SCOPE AND INTERPRETATION OF RIGHTS AND PRINCIPLES

1.   Any limitation on the exercise of the rights and freedoms recognised by this Charter must be provided for by

law and respect the essence of those rights and freedoms. Subject to the principle of proportionality, limitations may be made only if they are necessary and genuinely meet objectives of general interest recognised by the Union or the need to protect the rights and freedoms of others.

2.   Rights recognised by this Charter for which provision is made in other Parts of the Constitution shall be exercised under the conditions and within the limits defined by these relevant Parts

3.   Insofar as this Charter contains rights which correspond to rights guaranteed by the Convention for the Protection of Human Rights and Fundamental Freedoms, the meaning and scope of those rights shall be the same as those laid down by the said Convention. This provision shall not prevent Union law providing more extensive protection.

4.   Insofar as this Charter recognises fundamental rights as they result from the constitutional traditions common to the Member States, those rights shall be interpreted in harmony with those traditions.

5.   The provisions of this Charter which contain principles may be implemented by legislative and executive acts taken by Institutions and bodies of the Union, and by acts of Member States when they are implementing Union law, in the exercise of their respective powers. They shall be judicially cognisable only in the interpretation of such acts and in the ruling on their legality.

6.   Full account shall be taken of national laws and practices as specified in this Charter.

Article II-53   LEVEL OF PROTECTION

Nothing in this Charter shall be interpreted as restricting or adversely affecting human rights and fundamental freedoms as recognised, in their respective fields of application, by Union law and international law and by international agreements to which the Union or all the Member States are party, including the European Convention for the Protection of Human Rights and Fundamental Freedoms, and by the Member States' constitutions.

Article II-54   PROHIBITION OF ABUSE OF RIGHTS

Nothing in this Charter shall be interpreted as implying any right to engage in any activity or to perform any act aimed at the destruction of any of the rights and freedoms recognised in this Charter or at their limitation to a greater extent than is provided for herein.

PROTOCOL ON THE ROLE OF NATIONAL PARLIAMENTS IN THE EUROPEAN UNION

THE HIGH CONTRACTING PARTIES,

RECALLING that the way in which individual national Parliaments scrutinise their own governments in relation to the activities of the Union is a matter for the particular constitutional organisation and practice of each Member State,

DESIRING, however, to encourage greater involvement of national Parliaments in the activities of the European Union and to enhance their ability to express their views on legislative proposals as well as on other matters which may be of particular interest to them,

HAVE AGREED UPON the following provisions, which shall be annexed to the Constitution:

I. INFORMATION FOR MEMBER STATES' NATIONAL PARLIAMENTS

1. All Commission consultation documents (green and white papers and communications) shall be forwarded directly by the Commission to Member States' national Parliaments upon publication. The Commission shall also send Member States' national Parliaments the annual legislative programme as well as any other instrument of legislative planning or policy strategy that it submits to the European Parliament and to the Council of Ministers, at the same time as to those Institutions.

2.　　　　All legislative proposals sent to the European Parliament and to the Council of Ministers shall simultaneously be sent to Member States' national Parliaments.

3.　　　　Member States' national Parliaments may send to the Presidents of the European Parliament, the Council of Ministers and the Commission a reasoned opinion on whether a legislative proposal complies with the principle of subsidiarity, according to the procedure laid down in the Protocol on the application of the principles of subsidiarity and proportionality.

4.　　　　A six-week period shall elapse between a legislative proposal being made available by the Commission to the European Parliament, the Council of Ministers and the Member States' national Parliaments in the official languages of the European Union and the date when it is placed on an agenda for the Council of Ministers for adoption of a position under a legislative procedure, subject to exceptions on grounds of urgency, the reasons for which shall be stated in the act or position of the Council of Ministers. Save in urgent cases for which due reasons have been given, no agreement may be established on a legislative proposal during those six weeks. Ten days must elapse between the placing of a proposal on the agenda for the Council of Ministers and the adoption of a position of the Council of Ministers.

5.　　　　The agendas for and the outcome of meetings of the Council of Ministers, including the minutes of meetings where the Council of Ministers is deliberating on legislative proposals, shall be transmitted directly to Member States' national Parliaments, at the same time as to Member States' governments.

6.	When the European Council intends to make use of the provision of Article I-24(4), first subparagraph of the Constitution, national Parliaments shall be informed in advance.

When the European Council intends to make use of the provision of Article I-24(4), second subparagraph of the Constitution, national Parliaments shall be informed at least four months before any decision is taken.

7.	The Court of Auditors shall send its annual report to Member States' national Parliaments, for information, at the same time as to the European Parliament and to the Council of Ministers.

8.	In the case of bicameral national Parliaments, these provisions shall apply to both chambers.

II.	INTERPARLIAMENTARY COOPERATION

9.	The European Parliament and the national Parliaments shall together determine how interparliamentary cooperation may be effectively and regularly organised and promoted within the European Union.

10.   The Conference of European Affairs Committees may submit any contribution it deems appropriate for the attention of the European Parliament, the Council of Ministers and the Commission. That Conference shall in addition promote the exchange of information and best practice between Member States' Parliaments and the European Parliament, including their special committees. The Conference may also organise interparliamentary conferences on specific topics, in particular to debate matters of common foreign and security policy and of common security and defence policy. Contributions from the Conference shall in no way bind national Parliaments or prejudge their positions.

PROTOCOL ON THE APPLICATION OF THE PRINCIPLES OF SUBSIDIARITY AND PROPORTIONALITY

THE HIGH CONTRACTING PARTIES,

WISHING to ensure that decisions are taken as closely as possible to the citizens of the Union,

RESOLVED to establish the conditions for the application of the principles of subsidiarity and proportionality, as enshrined in Article I-9 of the Constitution, and to establish a system for monitoring the application of those principles by the Institutions,

HAVE AGREED UPON the following provisions, which shall be annexed to the Constitution:

1.   Each Institution shall ensure constant respect for the principles of subsidiarity and proportionality, as laid down in Article I-9 of the Constitution.

2.   Before proposing legislative acts, the Commission shall consult widely. Such consultations shall, where appropriate, take into account the regional and local dimension of the action envisaged. In cases of exceptional urgency, the Commission shall not conduct such consultations. It shall give reasons for the decision in its proposal.

3.   The Commission shall send all its legislative proposals and its amended proposals to the national Parliaments of the Member States at the same time as to the Union legislator. Upon adoption, legislative resolutions of the Euro-

pean Parliament and positions of the Council of Ministers shall be sent to the national Parliaments of the Member States.

4.   The Commission shall justify its proposal with regard to the principles of subsidiarity and proportionality. Any legislative proposal should contain a detailed statement making it possible to appraise compliance with the principles of subsidiarity and proportionality. This statement should contain some assessment of the proposal's financial impact and, in the case of a framework law, of its implications for the rules to be put in place by Member States, including, where necessary, the regional legislation. The reasons for concluding that a Union objective can be better achieved at Union level must be substantiated by qualitative and, wherever possible, quantitative indicators. The Commission shall take account of the need for any burden, whether financial or administrative, falling upon the Union, national governments, regional or local authorities, economic operators and citizens, to be minimised and commensurate with the objective to be achieved.

5.   Any national Parliament or any chamber of a national Parliament of a Member State may, within six weeks from the date of transmission of the Commission's legislative proposal, send to the Presidents of the European Parliament, the Council of Ministers and the Commission a reasoned opinion stating why it considers that the proposal in question does not comply with the principle of subsidiarity. It will be for each national Parliament or each chamber of a national Parliament to consult, where appropriate, regional parliaments with legislative powers.

6.   The European Parliament, the Council of Ministers and the Commission shall take account of the reasoned opinions issued by Member States' national Parliaments or by a chamber of a national Parliament.

The national Parliaments of Member States with unicameral Parliamentary systems shall have two votes, while each of the chambers of a bicameral Parliamentary system shall have one vote.

Where reasoned opinions on a Commission proposal's non-compliance with the principle of subsidiarity represent at least one third of all the votes allocated to the Member States' national Parliaments and their chambers, the Commission shall review its proposal. This threshold shall be at least a quarter in the case of a Commission proposal or an initiative emanating from a group of Member States under the provisions of Article III-165 of the Constitution on the area of freedom, security and justice.

After such review, the Commission may decide to maintain, amend or withdraw its proposal. The Commission shall give reasons for its decision.

7.   The Court of Justice shall have jurisdiction to hear actions on grounds of infringement of the principle of subsidiarity by a legislative act, brought in accordance with the rules laid down in Article III-270 of the Constitution by Member States, or notified by them in accordance with their

legal order on behalf of their national Parliament or a chamber of it.

In accordance with the same Article of the Constitution, the Committee of the Regions may also bring such actions as regards legislative acts for the adoption of which the Constitution provides that it be consulted.

8.		The Commission shall submit each year to the European Council, the European Parliament, the Council of Ministers and the national Parliaments of the Member States a report on the application of Article I-9 of the Constitution. This annual report shall also be forwarded to the Committee of the Regions and to the Economic and Social Committee.

PROTOCOL ON THE REPRESENTATION OF CITIZENS IN THE EUROPEAN PARLIAMENT AND THE WEIGHTING OF VOTES IN THE EUROPEAN COUNCIL AND THE COUNCIL OF MINISTERS

THE HIGH CONTRACTING PARTIES,

HAVE ADOPTED the following provisions, which shall be annexed to the Treaty establishing a Constitution for Europe:

Article 1   PROVISIONS CONCERNING THE
                EUROPEAN PARLAMENT

1.   Throughout the 2004-2009 parliamentary term, the number of representatives elected to the European Parliament in each Member State shall be as follows:

Belgium	24
Czech Republic	24
Denmark	14
Germany	99
Estonia	6
Greece	24
Spain	54
France	78
Ireland	13
Italy	78
Cyprus	6
Latvia	9
Lithuania	13
Luxembourg	6
Hungary	24
Malta	5

Netherlands	27
Austria	18
Poland	54
Portugal	24
Slovenia	7
Slovakia	14
Finland	14
Sweden	19
United Kingdom	78

Article 2 PROVISIONS CONCERNING THE WEIGHTING OF VOTES IN THE EUROPEAN COUNCIL AND THE COUNCIL OF MINISTERS

1. The following provisions shall remain in force until 1 November 2009, without prejudice to Article I-24 of the Constitution.

For deliberations of the European Council and of the Council of Ministers requiring a qualified majority, members' votes shall be weighted as follows:

Belgium	12
Czech Republic	12
Denmark	7
Germany	29
Estonia	4

Greece	12
Spain	27
France	29
Ireland	7
Italy	29
Cyprus	4
Latvia	4
Lithuania	7
Luxembourg	4
Hungary	12
Malta	3
Netherlands	13
Austria	10
Poland	27
Portugal	12
Slovenia	4
Slovakia	7
Finland	7
Sweden	10
United Kingdom	29

Decisions shall be adopted if there are at least 232 votes in favour representing a majority of the members where, under the Constitution, they must be adopted on a proposal from the Commission. In other cases decisions shall be adopted if there are at least 232 votes in favour representing at least two thirds of the members.

A member of the European Council or the Council of Ministers may request that, where a decision is taken by the European Council or the Council of Ministers by a qualified majority, a check is made to ensure that the Member States comprising the qualified majority represent at least 62 % of the total population of the Union. If that proves not to be the case, the decision shall not be adopted.

2.   For subsequent accessions, the threshold referred to in paragraph (1) shall be calculated to ensure that the qualified majority threshold expressed in votes does not exceed that resulting from the table in the Declaration on the enlargement of the European Union in the Final Act of the Conference which adopted the Treaty of Nice.

DECLARATION ATTACHED TO THE PROTOCOL ON THE REPRESENTATION OF CITIZENS IN THE EUROPEAN PARLIAMENT AND THE WEIGHTING OF VOTES IN THE EUROPEAN COUNCIL AND THE COUNCIL OF MINISTERS

The common position which will be taken by the Member States of the European Union at the conferences on the accession of Romania and/or Bulgaria regarding the allocation of seats in the European Parliament and the weighting of votes in the European Council and the Council of Ministers shall be as follows. If the accession to the European Union of Romania and/or Bulgaria takes place before the entry into force of the European Council decision foreseen in Article I-19(2) of the Constitution, the number of their elected representatives to the European Parliament shall be calculated on the basis of the figures of 33 and 17 respectively, corrected according to the same formula as that which determined the number of representatives in the European Parliament for each Member State as indicated in the Protocol on the representation of citizens in the European Parliament and the weighting of votes in the European Council and the Council of Ministers.

The Treaty of Accession to the European Union may, by way of derogation from Article I-19(2) of the Constitution, stipulate that the number of members of the European Parliament may temporarily exceed 736 for the remainder of the 2004 to 2009 Parliamentary term.

Without prejudice to Article I-24(2) of the Constitution, the weighting of the votes of Romania and Bulgaria in the European Council and the Council of Ministers shall be 14 and 10 respectively until 1 November 2009. At the time of each accession, the threshold referred to in the Protocol on the representation of citizens in the European Parliament and the weighting of votes in the European Council and the Council of Ministers shall be decided by the Council of Ministers.

LIST OF MEMBERS OF THE EUROPEAN CONVENTION

PRESIDENCY

Mr Valéry Giscard d'Estaing
Chairman

Mr Giuliano Amato
Vice-Chairman

Mr Jean-Luc Dehaene
Vice-Chairman

OTHER MEMBERS OF THE PRAESIDIUM

Mr Michel Barnier
Representative of the European Commission

Mr John Bruton
Representative of the National Parliaments

Mr Henning Christophersen
Representative of the Danish Presidency

Mr Alfonso Dastis
Representative of the Spanish Presidency
(from March 2003)

Mr Klaus Hänsch
Representative of the European Parliament

Mr Giorgos Katiforis
Representative of the Greek Presidency
(until February 2003)

Mr Iñigo Méndez De Vigo
Representative of the European Parliament

Ms Ana Palacio
Representative of the Spanish Presidency
(until March 2003)

Mr Giorgos Papandreou
Representative of the Greek Presidency
(from February 2003)

Ms Gisela Stuart
Representative of the National Parliaments

Mr Antonio Vitorino
Representative of the European Commission

Mr Alojz Peterle
Invitee

CONVENTION MEMBERS

REPRESENTATIVES OF THE EUROPEAN PARLIAMENT

Mr Jens-Peter Bonde (DK)
Mr Elmar Brok (D)
Mr Andrew Nicholas Duff (UK)
Mr Olivier Duhamel (F)
Mr Klaus Hänsch (D)
Ms Sylvia-Yvonne Kaufmann (D)
Mr Timothy Kirkhope (UK)
Mr Alain Lamassoure (F)
Ms Linda McAvan (UK)
Ms Hanja Maij-Weggen (NL)
Mr Luís Marinho (P)
Mr Íñigo Méndez De Vigo y Montojo (ES)
Ms Cristiana Muscardini (IT)
Mr Antonio Tajani (IT)
Ms Anne Van Lancker (B)
Mr Johannes Voggenhuber (ÖS)

REPRESENTATIVES OF THE COMMISSION

Mr Michel Barnier
Mr António Vitorino

REPRESENTATIVES OF THE MEMBER STATES

BELGIË/BELGIQUE

Government
Mr Louis Michel

National Parliament
Mr Karel de Gucht
Mr Elio di Rupo

DANMARK

Government
Mr Henning Christophersen

National Parlement
Mr Peter Skaarup
Mr Henrik dam Kristensen

DEUTSCHLAND

Government
Mr Joschka Fischer
replaced Mr Peter Glotz
in November 2002

National Parliament
Mr Jürgen Meyer
Mr Erwin Teufel

ΕΛΛΑΔΑ

Government
Mr Giorgos Papandreou
replaced Mr Giorgos Katiforis
in February 2003

National Parliament
Mr Paraskevas Avgerinos
Ms Marietta Giannakou

ESPAÑA

Government
Mr Alfonso Dastis
replaced Mr Carlos Bastarreche
as alternate member in
September 2002, then
Ms Ana Palacio as member
in March 2003

National Parliament
Mr Josep Borrell Fontelles
Mr Gabriel Cisneros Laborda

FRANCE

Government
Mr Dominique de Villepin
replaced Mr Pierre Moscovici
in November 2002

National Parliament
Mr Pierre Lequiller
replaced Mr Alain Barrau
in July 2002
Mr Hubert Haenel

IRELAND

Government
Mr Dick Roche
replaced Mr Ray MacSharry
in July 2002

National Parliament
Mr John Bruton
Mr Proinsias de Rossa

ITALIA

Government
Mr Gianfranco Fini

National Parliament
Mr Marco Follini
Mr Lamberto Dini

LUXEMBOURG

Government
Mr Jacques Santer

National Parliament
Mr Paul Helminger
Mr Ben Fayot

NEDERLAND

Government
Mr Gijs de Vries
replaced Mr Hans van Mierlo
in October 2002

National Parliament
Mr René van der Linden
Mr Frans Timmermans

ÖSTERREICH

Government
Mr Hannes Farnleitner

National Parliament
Mr Caspar Einem
Mr Reinhard Eugen Bösch

PORTUGAL

Government
Mr Ernâni Lopes
replaced Mr João de Vallera
in May 2002

National Parliament
Mr Alberto Costa
Ms Eduarda Azevedo

SUOMI/FINLAND

Government
Ms Teija Tiilikainen

National Parliament
Mr Kimmo Kiljunen
Mr Jari Vilén
replaced Mr Matti Vanhanen
in May 2003

SVERIGE

Government
Ms Lena Hjelm-Wallén

National Parliament
Mr Sören Lekberg
Mr Göran Lennmarker

UNITED KINGDOM

Government
Mr Peter Hain

National Parliament
Ms Gisela Stuart
Mr David Heathcoat-Amory

REPRESENTATIVES OF THE CANDIDATE COUNTRIES

Κὔπρος/CYPRUS

Government
Mr Michael Attalides

National Parliament
Ms Eleni Mavrou
Mr Panayiotis Demetriou

MALTA

Government
Mr Peter Serracino-Inglott

National Parliament
Mr Michael Frendo
Mr Alfred Sant

MAGYARORSZÀG/HUNGARY

Government
Mr Péter Balázs
replaced Mr János Martonyi
in June 2002

National Parliament
Mr József Szájer
Mr Pál Vastagh

POLSKA/POLAND

Government
Ms Danuta Hübner

National Parliament
Mr Jozef Oleksy
Mr Edmund Wittbrodt

ROMÂNIA/ROMANIA

Government
Ms Hildegard Carola
Puwak

National Parliament
Mr Alexandru Athanasiu
replaced Mr Liviu Maior
in February 2003
Mr Puiu Hasotti

SLOVENSKO/SLOVAKIA

Government
Mr Ivan Korčok
replaced Mr Ján Figel
in November 2002

National Parliament
Mr Jan Figel
replaced Mr Pavol Hamzik
in October 2002
Ms Irena Belohorská

LATVIJA/LATVIA

Government
Ms Sandra Kalniete
replaced Mr Roberts Zile
in January 2003

National Parliament
Mr Rihards Piks
Ms Liene Liepina
replaced Mr Edvins Inkēns
in January 2003

EESTI/ESTONIA

Government
Mr Lennart Meri

National Parliament
Mr Tunne Kelam
Mr Rein Lang
replaced Mr Peeter Reitzberg
in April 2003

LIETUVA/LITHUANIA

Government
Mr Rytis Martikonis

National Parliament
Mr Vytenis Andriukaitis
Mr Algirdas Gricius
in December 2002 replaced
Mr Alvydas Medalinskas,
who in turn replaced
Ms Dalia Kutraite-Giedraitiene
as alternate member

България/BULGARIA

Government
Ms Meglena Kuneva

National Parliament
Mr Daniel Valchev
Mr Nikolai Mladenov

ČESKÁ REPUBLIKA/CZECH REPUBLIC

Government
Mr Jan Kohout
replaced Mr Jan Kavan
in September 2002

National Parliament
Mr Jan Zahradil
Mr Josef Zieleniec

SLOVENIJA/SLOVENIA

Government

Mr Dimitrij Rupel
replaced Mr Matjaz Nahtigal
in January 2003

National Parliament

Mr Jelko Kacin
replaced Mr Slavko Gaber
in January 2003

Mr Alojz Peterle

TÜRQÍYE/TURKEY

Government

Mr Abdullah Gül
in March 2003 replaced
Mr Yasar Yakis, who had replaced
Mr Mesut Yilmaz
in December 2002

National Parliament

Mr Zekeriya Akcam
replaced Mr Ali Tekin
in December 2002

Mr Kemal Derviş
replaced Ms Ayfer Yilmaz
in December 2002

ALTERNATES

REPRESENTATIVES OF THE EUROPEAN PARLIAMENT

Mr William Abitbol (F)
Ms Almeida Garrett (P)
Mr John Cushnahan (IRL)
Ms Lone Dybkjaer (DK)
Ms Pervenche Berès (F)
Ms Maria Berger (ÖS)
Mr Carlos Carnero González (ES)
Mr Neil MacCormick (UK)
Ms Piia-Noora Kauppi (FI)
Ms Elena Paciotti (IT)
Mr Luís Queiró (P)
Mr Reinhard Rack (ÖS)
Mr Esko Seppänen (FI)
The Earl of Stockton (UK)
Ms Helle Thorning-Schmidt (DK)
Mr Joachim Wuermeling (D)

REPRESENTATIVES OF THE COMMISSION

Mr David O'Sullivan
Mr Paolo Ponzano

REPRESENTATIVES
OF THE MEMBER STATES

BELGIË/BELGIQUE

Government
Mr Pierre Chevalier

National Parliament
Mr Danny Pieters
Ms Marie Nagy

DANMARK

Government
Mr Poul Schlüter

National Parliament
Mr Per Dalgaard
Mr Niels Helveg Petersen

DEUTSCHLAND

Government
Mr Hans Martin Bury
replaced Mr Gunter Pleuger
in November 2002

National Parliament
Mr Peter Altmaier
Mr Wolfgang Gerhards
replaced Mr Wolfgang Senff
in March 2003

ΕΛΛΑΔΑ

Government
Mr Giorgos Katiforis
replaced Mr Panayiotis Ioakimidis
in February 2003

National Parliament
Mr Nikolaos Constantopoulos
Mr Evripidis Stiliniadis

ESPAÑA

Government
Ms Ana Palacio
replaced Mr Alfonso Dastis
in March 2003

National Parliament
Mr Diego López Garrido
Mr Alejandro Muñoz Lonso

FRANCE

Government
Ms Pascale Andreani
replaced Mr Pierre Vimont
in August 2002

National Parliament
Mr Jacques Floch
replaced Ms Anne-Marie Idrac
in July 2002
Mr Robert Badinter

IRELAND

Government
Mr Bobby McDonagh

National Parliament
Mr Pat Carey
replaced Mr Martin Cullen
in July 2002
Mr John Gormley

ITALIA

Government
Mr Francesco E. Speroni

National Parliament
Mr Valdo Spini
Mr Filadelfio Guido Basile

LUXEMBOURG

Government
Mr Nicolas Schmit

National Parliament
Mr Gaston Giberyen
Ms Renée Wagener

NEDERLAND

Government
Mr Thom de Bruijn

National Parliament
Mr Wim van Eekelen
Mr Jan Jacob van Dijk
replaced Mr Hans van Baalen
in October 2002

ÖSTERREICH

Government
Mr Gerhard Tusek

National Parliament
Ms Evelin Lichtenberger
Mr Eduard Mainoni
replaced Mr Gerhard Kurzmann
in March 2003

PORTUGAL

Government
Mr Manuel Lobo Antunes

National Parliament
Mr Guilherme d'Oliveira Martins
replaced Mr Osvaldo de Castro in June 2002
Mr António Nazaré Pereira

SUOMI/FINLAND

Government
Mr Antti Peltomäki

National Parliament
Mr Hannu Takkula
replaced Ms Riitta Korhonen in May 2003
Mr Esko Helle

SVERIGE

Government
Mr Sven-Olof Petersson
replaced Ms Lena Hallengren in December 2002

National Parliament
Mr Kenneth Kvist
Mr Ingvar Svensson

UNITED KINGDOM

Government
Baroness Scotland of Asthal

National Parliament
Lord Tomlinson
Lord Maclennan of Rogart

REPRESENTATIVES OF THE CANDIDATE COUNTRIES

Κὔπρος/CYPRUS

Government	*National Parliament*
Mr Theophilos V. Theophilou	Mr Marios Matsakis
	Ms Androula Vassiliou

MALTA

Government	*National Parliament*
Mr John Inguanez	Ms Dolores Cristina
	Mr George Vella

MAGYARORSZÀG/HUNGARY

Government	*National Parliament*
Mr Péter Gottfried	Mr András Kelemen
	Mr István Szent-Iványi

POLSKA/POLAND

Government	*National Parliament*
Mr Janusz Trzciński	Ms Marta Fogler
	Ms Genowefa Grabowska

ROMÂNIA/ROMANIA

Government
Mr Constantin Ene
replaced Mr Ion Jinga
in December 2002

National Parliament
Mr Péter Eckstein-Kovacs
Mr Adrian Severin

SLOVENSKO/SLOVAKIA

Government
Mr Juraj Migaš

National Parliament
Ms Zuzana Martinakova
replaced Mr Frantisek Sebej
in November 2002

Mr Boris Zala
replaced Ms Olga Keltosova
in November 2002

LATVIJA/LATVIA

Government
Mr Roberts Zile
replaced Mr Guntars Krasts
in January 2003

National Parliament
Mr Guntars Krasts
replaced Mr Maris Sprindzuks
in January 2003

Mr Arturs Krisjanis Karins
replaced Ms Inese Birzniece
in January 2003

EESTI/ESTONIA

Government
Mr Henrik Hololei

National Parliament
Ms Liina Tõnisson
replaced Ms Liia Hänni
in April 2003

Mr Urmas Reinsalu
replaced Mr Ülo Tärno
in April 2003

LIETUVA/LITHUANIA

Government
Mr Oskaras Jusys

National Parliament
Mr Gintautas Šivickas
in February 2003 replaced
Mr Gediminas Dalinkevicius,
who had replaced
Mr Rolandas Pavilionis
in December 2002

Mr Eugenijus Maldeikis
replaced Mr Alvydas Medalinskas
in February 2003

България/BULGARIA

Government
Ms Neli Kutskova

National Parliament
Mr Alexander Arabadjiev
Mr Nesrin Uzun

ČESKÁ REPUBLIKA/CZECH REPUBLIC

Government
Ms Lenka Anna Rovna
replaced Mr Jan Kohout
in September 2002

National Parliament
Mr Petr Nečas
Mr František Kroupa

SLOVENIJA/SLOVENIA

Government
Mr Janez Lenarčič

National Parliament
Mr Franc Horvat
replaced Ms Danica Simšič
in January 2003
Mr Mihael Brejc

TÜRQÍYE/TURKEY

Government
M. Oğuz Demiralp
replaced Mr Nihat Akyol
in August 2002

National Parliament
M. Ibrahim Özal
replaced Mr Kürsat Eser
in December 2002

M. Necdet Budak
replaced Mr A. Emre Kocaoglou
in December 2002

OBSERVERS

Mr Roger Briesch
Economic and Social Committee

Mr Josef Chabert
Committee of the Regions

Mr João Cravinho
European Social Partners

Mr Manfred Dammeyer
Committee of the Regions

Mr Patrick Dewael
Committee of the Regions

Mr Nikiforos Diamandouros
European Ombudsman (replaced Mr Jacob Söderman in March 2003)

Ms Claude Du Granrut
Committee of the Regions

Mr Göke Daniel Frerichs
Economic and Social Committee

Mr Emilio Gabaglio
European Social Partners

Mr Georges Jacobs
European Social Partners

Mr Claudio Martini
Committee of the Regions

Ms Anne-Maria Sigmund
Economic and Social Committee

Mr Ramón Luis Valcárcel Siso
Committee of the Regions (replaced Mr Eduardo Zaplana in February 2003;
Ms Eva-Riitta Siitonen had acted as alternate since October 2002)

SECRETARIAT

Sir John Kerr
Secretary-General

Ms Annalisa Giannella
Deputy Secretary-General

Ms Marta Arpio Santacruz

Ms Agnieszka Bartol

Mr Hervé Bribosia

Ms Nicole Buchet

Ms Élisabeth Gateau

Ms Maryem van den Heuvel

Mr Clemens Ladenburger

Ms Maria José Martínez Iglesias

Mr Nikolaus Meyer Landrut

Mr Guy Milton

Mr Ricardo Passos

Ms Kristin de Peyron

Mr Alain Pilette

Mr Alan Piotrowski

Mr Étienne de Poncins

Ms Alessandra Schiavo

Ms Walpurga Speckbacher

TABLE OF CONTENTS

European Convention

Draft treaty establishing a Constitution for Europe, submitted to the European Council meeting in Thessaloniki – 20 June 2003

Luxembourg: Office for Official Publications of the European Communities

2003 – VIII–161 pp. – 12 x 18 cm

ISBN 92-78-40171-4